A Rhyme in Time

Rhythm, Speech Activities and Improvisation for the Classroom
by Doug Goodkin

Editor: Debbie Cavalier

Consulting Editor: Peter Greenwood

Book Cover & Layout: Jorge Paredes

Photographs: Doug Goodkin, The San Francisco School

FOREWORD

Doug Goodkin's, *A Rhyme in Time,* with Orff-Schulwerk extensions, sails on welcome wings to both classroom and music teacher's libraries, blurring the curriculum lines, and treating language, music, and movement as "fingers on the same hand." This uncommonly pragmatic collection, insouciant in spirit and wise in direction, suggests clever and developmentally sound ways to extend a host of musical experiences rhythmically, tonally, and in movement; yet always includes the invitation to the student and teacher to shape the process. This trusting and respectful way of offering materials, i.e. as uncompleted tasks which can travel in many directions, engenders great motivation to explore the ideas abundant in this book, and is wholly in keeping with the philosophy found in the Orff-Schulwerk approach.

Organized in a visually logical format, succinct and clear, *A Rhyme in Time* uses both familiar and lesser known rhymes from diverse cultures as "starting points." The attention in particular to the English strand of rhymes, will most certainly resuscitate interest in using these delightful, musically useful, and ageless departures. That the activities at times demand more advanced musical skills and coordination, illustrates how easily Orff-Schulwerk techniques can adapt to all ages and abilities.

Finally, there is a bonus to the alert reader, found in choice excerpts from the *literati,* and in the droll asides of this witty, articulate, and thinking musician/music educator, Doug Goodkin.

Judith Thomas, 1997

CONTENTS

INTRODUCTION

This little piggy went to market . . . Remember those fingers pinching your toes, the tingling in your body as you anticipated the exciting *Weeee-weee-weee* as the last pig ran home? Probably none of us ever thought about the strangeness of a pig eating roast beef or wondered why that last pig ran home. We were in a world of enchantment, soothed and stimulated by the musical voice of our mother and the warmth of her touch. Without knowing it, we were being taught that language was more than the practical "hot," the scientific "flower," the moral "No!"—it was a world of pure play and delight. Because we were held and touched, bounced and moved as we soaked up the sounds of rhymed speech, we would later be touched by the elegance of a finely spun poem or moved by a well-turned phrase.

> *I wanted to write poetry in the beginning because I had fallen in love with words. The first poems I knew were nursery rhymes, and before I could read them for myself, I had come to love just the words of them, the words alone. What the words stood for, symbolized, or meant was of very secondary importance. What mattered was the sound of them . . . I cared for the shapes of sound that their names made in my ears . . . for the colors the words cast on my eyes.*
>
> -Dylan Thomas

Those experiences in language are the beginning of our journey into literacy. They also set us on the road towards music. The poet, songwriter, orator and musician alike learn their first lessons from two mothers—their own and, in the English-speaking world, Mother Goose. How can we move from the mother's knee to our alma mater and stay connected with our Mother Goose origins? How do rhythmic rhymes nurture both literacy and musicality? This book hopes to explore these questions, give some hints as to how "Dickery, dickery, dare" can lead to Dickens, "Baa baa black sheep" to Bach.

TO THE MUSIC TEACHER

The activities offered here use language as a means of musical development. They were inspired by the practice of Orff-Schulwerk and are based on Carl Orff's perception that speech is a natural way to enter music for the young child. Rhymes and poems build a foundation for rhythm, phrase, and form from which an understanding of the more abstract aspects of music may be built.

What is the connection between music and language? The most important link is simply that they both enter through the ear. As such, attention to nuance of rhythm, pitch, timbre and phrase is common to both. This common ground, though ultimately leading to different ends, can be mined in our early experiences in music and throughout our musical growth.

Though they remain connected through song, music and language do part company early on as they move toward their own proper craft. Nevertheless, it is clear that the language that succeeds best, whether it be poetry or a political speech, is that which has retained a certain musicality, rhythm, timbre, phrase, cadence and form. Likewise, the music that succeeds best is that which communicates in the manner of the best language, speaking directly to the heart, the jazzman's plea "Hear me talkin' to ya."

As music teachers, we're entrusted with leading each child's innate sense of rhythm towards an understanding of rhythm's many facets. We're asked to lead the natural love of song towards the intricacies of melody and harmony. We're challenged to tune the ear to timbre and turn the mind toward form. Orff has shown us that rhymes will help us in these tasks by bringing the abstractions of music down to the ground of the young child's love affair with language. How can we spin the thread of musical development from the raw material of rhymes?

Rhythm: Rhymes are rich in rhythm. All rhymes are grounded in beat, meter, duration values and phrasing. Specific rhythmic elements can be learned from certain rhymes; "Johnny Works with One Hammer" solidifies the experience of beat, "Bate Bate Chocolate" clarifies the relationship of quarter and eighth notes, "Pease Porridge Hot" introduces rests, "Roses Are Red" highlights phrases and "Whoops! Johnny" explores various meters. All poems may be notated with the children after the experience to solidify the connection between word rhythm and traditional rhythmic notation.

Melody: Nursery rhymes are traditionally spoken, but some have been set to existing folk melodies ("Twinkle, Twinkle Little Star", "Baa Baa Black Sheep," and "ABC" are all sung to the French folk song "Ah, vous dirai-je, Maman"). In this collection, the emphasis is on the spoken tradition, with attention to pitch variation (as in "Whoops! Johnny" and "Wee Willie Winkie") and the expressive speech that prepares both good singing and melodic contour.

Harmony: Numerous examples of multiple texture are given that use devices such as complementary ostinati ("Pin Marin") and canon ("Tantos Rios").

Timbre/Orchestration: Instrumental timbres that approximate vowels and consonants are explored in "Pease Porridge Hot," dynamic comes into play in "Tie My Shoe" and "Bate Bate Chocolate" and instrumental qualities are integral to "Wee Willie Winkie." Orchestrating the various timbres includes thickening of texture in "Johnny Works with One Hammer" while "Man In Car" offers a complex orchestration made simple through language cue.

Exploring various orchestral devices from the base of rhymes is one of the unique features of this approach—it extends the work begun on the mother's knee and moves it towards new levels of musical understanding.

Form: The structures of the various rhymes suggest a variety of musical forms. Students may explore a number of variations—transferring words to body percussion or instruments, internalizing the text while moving, improvising through a phrase and then combining ideas to create simple forms.

This work suggests that the rhyme is one of the most accessible and effective means of engaging young children in creative music-making: they can move with ease from the known (the language of words) to the unknown (the language of music); the imagery of the texts captures their imagination more readily than abstract explanations of the principles of music; the meaning of the words translates to the sensation of sounds and renders those sounds more meaningful; finally, the playful approach to transforming rhymes into music by following and internalizing the structure of the texts allows for some satisfying and complex pieces which would be impossible to teach any other way. (Try having students read a score of "Man in Car" and note the difference). Most importantly, they are involved in every step of the creative process rather than being passive players of a composer's score or a teacher's lesson plan.

That these rhymes are a central feature of dynamic music education has been made evident by the children's response and the impressive results. And though as music teachers we turn the rhymes toward musical goals, we should also be aware of how this work serves the child's language development. Some of the benefits of this awareness are:

• A music teacher able to explain to parents, school boards and fellow teachers precisely how musical experiences aid language and mathematical development will broaden their understanding of music's contribution to the overall school curriculum. Not only does music give our children a way to speak without words and feel the order of pattern without number, it can lead them to greater understanding of both words and numbers.

• Knowing these connections helps us integrate our work with our fellow classroom teachers. Ideally the language arts teacher and the music teacher will collaborate, using the same rhyme or activity, each focusing on his or her chosen field. (For a good example of this, *Working the Word* by Judy Thomas and Susan Katz.)

• Our primary mission as teachers is not necessarily to teach music, but to teach the child through the vehicle of music. How satisfying to know that the work we do helps nurture all of their intelligences. It is not just musical intelligence that is awakened and trained, but logical/mathematical through the inherent patterning of music, visual/spatial through working with intervals on xylophones and dance in space, kinesthetic through experiencing every concept in the body, intrapersonal through the improvising, composing and expressing oneself through sound and movement, interpersonal through the intense social demands of group dance and music-making—and linguistic through song, poetry and rhymes.* The more aware we are of these potentials, the more consciously we can bring them out in these activities and serve the whole child.

* These named intelligences reference Howard Gardner's definitions from his book: *Frames of Mind.*

TO THE CLASSROOM TEACHER

A narrow definition of literacy would be "having the ability to read and write." But to be literate in the broadest sense means to be fully educated, cultured and knowledgeable of literature. Both definitions fit the school curriculum now called "language arts." The "arts" half of that term suggests that one of our goals is to promote an appreciation of the world's great poetry and prose. This, in turn, implies a broadening of our definition of literature. The Hindu epics *The Ramayana* and *The Mahabharata,* passed on through the theater arts of the South Indian *Kathakali* drama and the Javanese *Wayang Kulit* shadow play, might be considered literature, as might the sung Spanish romances or the chanted Navajo epics. By including these oral forms of poetry and storytelling, we imply a literacy that reaps the full gifts of our language potential.

> *The vitality of our language resides as much in the sound of our words and beat of their rhythms as in their meanings. That's why Lorca puts the poetry of "duende" together with song, dance, and bull-fighting, and that's why poems belong more to speaking than reading, more to passionate declamation and ecstatic jubilation . . . than to typed lines on bleached paper. Good language asks to be spoken aloud, mind to mind and heart to heart, by embodied voices that . . . still delight in savoring vowels and the clipped spitting of explosive consonants.*
>
> -James Hillman

When we tune our ears to rhythm, rhyme, sound and story, we gain a deeper access to our rich inheritance of both oral and written language. The love of sound can help inspire the deciphering of symbol, the play of rhythm and rhyme can help lead to the work of rules. Nursery rhymes in the home and later in the school prepare all this fertile ground. A brief look at some of the components of language will show how.

- **Sound:** Developmental psychologists and poets alike affirm that sound precedes sense. All subsequent love for and facility in language comes from our initial enchantment with the music of speech.

> *What we do get in life and miss so often in literature is the sentence sounds that underlie the words. Words in themselves do not convey meaning . . . the sound of them does.*
>
> -Robert Frost

Nursery rhymes are rich in sound; "Jack and Jill," "Lucy Locket," "Peter Peter," "Pease Porridge," "Pocos Puentes" and "Wee Willie Winkie" all set the young speaker down the garden path of alliteration. The work of phonetics is greatly enriched by Mother Goose (make your own list: Betty Botter, Davy Dumpling, Goosey Gander, Simple Simon and a host of other colorful consonant characters!).

• **Rhyme:** Rhyme is a key component in the delicious music of nursery lore. As the ear tunes to "Bate Bate Chocolate," "Peter Peter Pumpkin Eater," and "Lucy Locket" (who) lost her pocket, the play of language comes to the forefront. The activities which highlight rhyming words through movement, percussion or silence turn our awareness to their place in the structure. The child's own vocabulary of rhymes will grow through these and other examples. I often teach the rhymes by leaving out key rhyming words and inviting the children to fill them in. Free verse has its place in poetry, but children love and need rhymes—especially in their beginning stages.

• **Rhythm:** Each game herein provides many possibilities: the music teacher may use the words to teach rhythmic durations while the classroom teacher may use the same exercise for teaching syllabic construction. Rhythm will also prove an aid to memory in reciting poetry and a general help in reading, expressing the flow and cadence of language. Although most of the rhymes here are tied strongly to beat and meter— crucial to coherent musical expression—the language reader will eventually aim for a more fluid effect, varying tempo and shading rhythms. The activity given with "Wee Willie Winkie" is an example of this freer kind of rhythm. (Music has its moments of rubato or free tempo also, but usually depends on a steady beat.)

• **Imagery:** *The cow jumped over the moon . . . the dish ran away with the spoon.*
  Five geese in a flock . . . sit and sing, by a spring.
  Rings on her fingers and bells on her toes . . .
Such delicious images in these rhymes! The young child's dreamlike world is given an even greater vibrancy by the color in these word pictures. Years later, this experience with alliteration and imagery will re-surface reading Gerard Manley Hopkins:

. . . skies of couple-colour as a brinded cow; rose-moles all in stipple upon trout that swim . . .

Compare that to some contemporary children's songs:

Oh, you walk and you walk and you walk and you stop!
Touch your shoulders, touch your knees, raise your arms and drop them please.

Gone is the fancy, the music, the poetry! The children fed on this diet will grow up to be good respectable citizens who read their newspaper, but they will miss one of the great gifts of language—its capacity to evoke fantastic imagery.

- **Sense:** Here we have arrived at the muscle of words— their sense and meaning. Now they part company with music, which can never mean something in the way that "cat," "practice" and "existentialism" do. Now we're in the realm of practical learning. "Where did Dick and Jane go?" "Who is Puff?" "Why did they name the dog Spot?" These beginning steps at interpretive reading and critical thinking are an important part of the work offered here. Every rhyme, poem and song, whether performed in the classroom or the music class, is an opportunity for analysis and discussion. The poem "Yes Papa" offers an opportunity for spirited argument—that it implies more than one meaning is wonderful news for future literary analysis. "Man in Car" offers a moral, but it is somewhat hidden in the text; both of these poems communicate through story.

- **Story:** The stories in the rhymes offer many possibilities for elaboration—"Why did Jack and Jill need water? What happened after they tumbled down? Why was the well on top of the hill?" But the rhymes offer another kind of story—the story behind the rhymes. This ranges from new words (What is a clinker? What is a chimney pot?) to an inquiry about the Black Plague (save this for the older kids!).

- **Syntax:** No matter how delightful our introduction to language, we all eventually come up against the hard wall of grammar. But rhymes can help us keep our sense of humor— "Man in Car," for example, offers a musical way to isolate parts of speech. For a refreshing approach to a difficult task, try creating a musical score from a diagrammed sentence!

• **Reading Skills:** Having played with phonemes and syllables, rhymes and phrases, we arrive at the specific task of literacy—reading and writing Having lived with the rhymes in the oral realm, reading them in print and writing them down is a wonderful extension that falls squarely in the realm of the classroom teacher (the music teacher has other tasks in mind). This organic method of drawing from the child's experience has been proven to be a great motivator and connection-maker. It need not replace a set reading series, but it will certainly deepen the child's experience of words and ideas.

• **Music in the Classroom:** Though the preceding remarks address the rhyme games in terms of what they offer language development, the classroom teacher will derive satisfaction knowing that he or she is supporting the child's musical development as well. With no formal musical background, theoretical knowledge or instrumental training, any teacher with a good sense of time can help awaken beat and rhythm in the children with the help of these activities. As schools employ fewer arts specialists so important to the child's development, it becomes increasingly important for the classroom teacher to offer a taste of this valuable training.* And in schools with music specialists, teachers need not be concerned about duplicating class plans because each brings a unique spirit to the activity and each will aim its extensions in a different direction.

---

* While simultaneously lobbying for such arts specialists! The classroom teacher can't be expected to teach music any more than the music teacher can be expected to teach reading.

THE ACTIVITIES:

Open structures for movement, body percussion, unpitched percussion.

The games herein offer open structures that acquaint students with the process of developing music and movement skills through language. These processes suggest that many mediums are interchangeable; we can speak the words, play their rhythm on our body, move to and with that rhythm, transfer it to percussion, metamorphose speech to song—the permutations are inexhaustible! By moving through these processes repeatedly with a variety of rhymes and poems, children learn how music can be created from speech, how it can be extended, transposed, set into form and given life through performance.

This type of work can serve the creative process, but there is also a danger—we must beware of putting every rhyme or poem indiscriminately through a mill that gives everything the flavor of processed cheese. By asking, "What does this poem want to do? Which of the myriad possibilities does its text and structure suggest?", we keep our work truly creative and avoid mere cleverness and pedagogy. Just as we strive to know the distinct personality of each student, so might we try to know the unique character of each poem. Of course, poems, like people, have complex, multi-dimensional personalities— there are always many answers to the question "What does this poem want to do?" I've suggested certain directions here, but other qualities may surface for you and the children —and should be most heartily welcomed!

A book of nursery rhymes may seem to suggest activities for the preschool child, but these games cut across all age levels—from 3 years old to 103! The open structures are adaptable to the skill level of any group (and equally to the different levels within each group). This book presupposes enough teaching experience to adjust the range and pace of activities. Part of the joy is in discovering how a rhyme just right for a three-year-old can be extended far enough musically to challenge a graduate music student! Yet text does matter. Finding age-appropriate texts is one of the great challenges to music and language teachers. The older children will tell you immediately if a rhyme seems "babyish" while the younger ones will let you know through restlessness or boredom when a text is over their head.

Text is always best taught aurally, though in many cases a written version is useful to clarify the words or reinforce reading skills. It may also serve as a score, with key words highlighted (as in "Man in Car" and "Bate Bate Chocolate"). But even when a written score is used, the goal should be memorization, freeing the body and mind to devote full attention to musical and kinesthetic expression.

The majority of the rhymes herein are from the Mother Goose collection. They celebrate our country's parent tongue, English, and are themselves a part of the body of English literature. However, in today's American classroom, rhymes in other languages are a welcome addition, both as an affirmation of our diverse cultural backgrounds and as an expansion of our musical language. I have included a few Spanish poems as a taste of this kind of work, but have reserved the fuller collection for another volume.

These activities are offered with a music focus and a language focus, both of which are flexible—you may choose to highlight a different aspect of the rhyme's potential. The variations suggested tend to move the poems towards musical goals and the classroom extensions towards language, but again, these are flexible suggestions—both may happen in either classroom. Our hope is to soften the borders of each specialty without losing the valuable definition those borders provide.

Playing with speech is a joy for everyone. Watch the children's faces light up as they experience *A Rhyme in Time!*

ONE-TWO, TIE MY SHOE

One - two, tie my shoe, three - four, shut the door, five - six,

pick up sticks, seven-eight, lay them straight, nine - ten, a big fat hen!

Music focus: Opposites (high—low, loud—soft, long—short)

Quarter/eighth notes

Language focus: Rhyme

Antonyms

Activities:

• Speak each phrase, leave out rhyming word and invite children to fill it in. (If no answer is forthcoming or it's "wrong," fill it in yourself.)

• Children mime actions (tie shoes, shut door).

• Say the numbers of the poem in a high voice and the words in a low voice. Repeat with loud and soft. Use matching gestures (arms high/low, arms extended in front/held close to the chest) and appropriate facial expressions.*

High Voice - "One-Two, Tie My Shoe"   Low Voice - "One-Two, Tie My Shoe"

• Continue exploring contrasts, doing one thing with the numbers and a different thing with the words, e.g.: smooth/choppy; fast/slow; speak/sing; speak/silent; nice/mean; excited/bored; pat/clap; sit/stand; move/freeze; Valley girl/Oxford English professor.

*If your eyebrows don't raise with your high voice and frown with your low voice, your students may grow up to be TV Newscasters!

Variations:

- Half the group performs the numbers with one quality, the other half performs the words with a contrasting quality.

- Mix the qualities, one pair per stanza, e.g.: hi/low for *one—two tie my shoe*, soft/loud for *three—four, shut the door.*

- Gradually change qualities, e.g.: begin soft with *one—two, tie my shoe* and crescendo to loud by *nine—ten, a big fat hen.*

- Transfer text to unpitched percussion, e.g.: play numbers on bells, words on drums (I enjoy the unchanging archetypal rhythm of the first four stanzas— ♩ ♩ ♫ ♩ — contrasted with the final phrase beginning with an upbeat—*a big fat hen!* I have adapted the more traditional *buckle* for *tie* to achieve consistency and "cheated" on that troublesome number "seven" [the only two syllable number in the first ten!] by playing one beat while saying two).

Classroom Extensions:

- Introduce or supplement the activity with a picture book on opposites. (*Nice and Nasty* by Nick Butterworth and Mick Inkpen, *Quick as a Cricket* by Audrey Wood—see your local children's librarian for other ideas.)

- Create a new text: *One—two, what shall I do? three—four, give money to the poor . . .*

- Create a new text in another language: *Uno—dos, caballos, tres—cuatro, hola gato . . .*

Comments:

This is often the first poem I do with three year olds. I love the clear contrast between numbers and words, which beautifully introduces the expressive range of our entire musical study. Working with opposites defines the parameters of the musical language; it sets the stage for what we can and can't do, summarized in what I feel as one of the cardinal rules of art: "Anything is permissible, but it must be contained by form and aesthetics."

Three-year-olds learning to cope with school rules— "no running in the classroom, no shouting, and so on" come to music class and discover that they <u>can</u> shout and they <u>can</u> run in class (is that why they love music class so much?), but—and it's a bold **but**—it must be contained in a form. They must shout the particular rhythm of the words at the right time and then instantly come back down to a whisper; they can run the length of the phrase *one—two*, but must freeze instantly on *tie my shoe*.

Art allows us to express feelings generally inappropriate in public—intense anger, exuberant ecstasy, wrenching grief—through the filter of musical tones, choreographed dance, paint, and poetry. The heat of those feelings is tempered in the structure of artistic form, cooled by the touch of aesthetics. By playing with opposite qualities in activities like these, students can be freed from having to identify with one or the other. Shy kids can explore the empowerment of shouting, wild aggressive kids can come to know the calm of a whisper. This is one of the great gifts of art, essential to our healthy development and available to the three-year-old joyfully chanting *One—two, tie my shoe!*

WHOOPS! JOHNNY

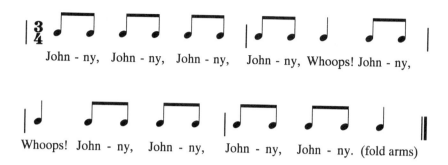

John - ny, John - ny, John - ny, John - ny, Whoops! John - ny,

Whoops! John - ny, John - ny, John - ny, John - ny. (fold arms)

Music focus: Hocket

Meter

Canon

Language focus: Syllables

Activities:

- Hold left hand with palm toward face. Touch the pinky with the pointer finger of the right hand. Moving to the left, touch each finger in turn while reciting *Johnny.* Slide finger between pointer finger and thumb of left hand for *Whoops!,* touch thumb for *Johnny* and reverse direction with another *Whoops!* sliding back up to pointer finger. After returning to the starting point (pinky of left hand), fold arms. I enjoy telling students that there's a "trick" at the end—they have to guess what it is. (The trick is I fold my arms at the end of each playing and announce how many other children have figured out the trick. I also ask those that have to help me notice who else is catching on.) Each time we return to the text, we'll try one of the variations to keep things interesting. If some still don't "get it" after five to ten play-ings, we may exaggerate the ending a bit.

Variations:

- Speak text with different qualities: fast/slow, low voice/high voice, whisper/shout, legato/staccato, etc. (see opposites: "Tie My Shoe," "Second Story Window")

- Use a contrasting quality for *Whoops!* e.g.: whisper *Johnny*, shout *Whoops!*, fast *Johnny*, slow *Whoops!*

• Use names from your group instead of Johnny or common names from other cultures
— Mohammed, Hans, Katherina, Tomoko.

• Switch hands; touch fingers with a different body part: chin, elbow, nose.

• Skip selected fingers.

• Slide between each finger, a different sound for each slide.

• In circle formation, everyone holds left hand up with fingers spread and plays on the hand of the person to the right.

• Begin and end on a different finger (*Whoops!* falls in a different place).

• All *Johnny's* silent, *Whoops!* out loud; add another *Whoops!* for folding arms.

• Combine last two variations: everyone chooses a finger to start on, *Johnny* silent, *Whoops!* out loud; all end on *Whoops!*

• Partners create their own variations and share with the group.

• Notate the rhythm of the text, introducing or reviewing quarter and eighth notes:

• Set in other meters, accenting words that fall on a pat.

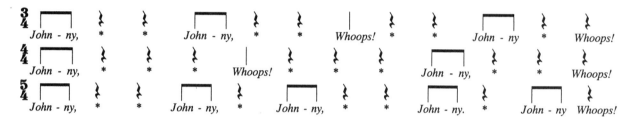

• Three groups, one per meter, reciting only accented word—all end on *Whoops!*

• Transfer text to body percussion: pat *Johnny*, clap *Whoops!*

• Reverse above.

• Augmentation: say and play rhyme twice as slow; diminution: twice as fast.

• Four part canon: each group enters after two beats.

• Transfer last five variations to unpitched percussion.

WHOOPS! JOHNNY—PERCUSSION PIECE

I. Layer in each of the following three meters

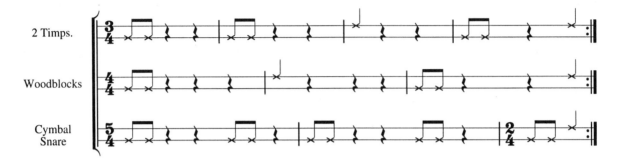

II. Add body percussion parts over above and create a choreography.

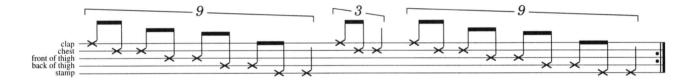

III. Play text in normal, augmented and diminished forms.

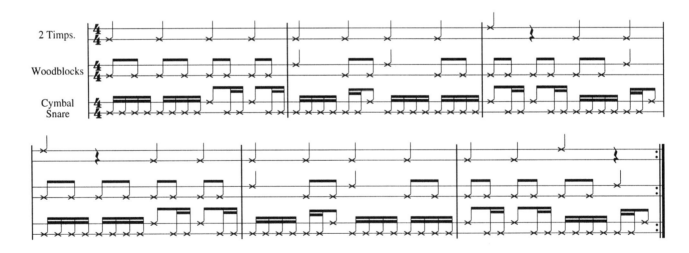

IV. Add body percussion as above and perform in 4-part canon.

V. Determine meeting point of all parts. End with all reciting rhyme on fingers.

Comments:

I have used this rhyme at workshops I've presented throughout the United States, Canada, Europe and Australia—the simple language makes it an ideal international text. It never fails to evoke astonishment at how much is possible with such a simple rhyme! The variations given proceed from simple to complex, ending with a piece that gathers some of the threads into a complex percussion piece for the older grades. It would be fun to perform at a concert and then lead the audience back to the original rhyme for infants!

It is not necessary to go through the entire sequence. Pick and choose from the variations offered, spread them out over time, add new ones and most importantly, invite the students to create more and share their ideas. I have given this task to students working as partners in classes and workshops and have never found a single idea exactly repeated! Brainstorming variations demonstrates clearly the endless possibilities of human creativity and can be a liberating revelation for the teacher (or student) accustomed to concrete cut-and-dry material. Once we realize how much is possible with what is close at hand, the energy shifts from product to process.

Understanding the possibilities of variation is essential—the kind of rigorous training that Bach undertook in his "Goldberg Variations" and Charlie Parker in his many pieces and improvisations based on Gershwin's "I Got Rhythm." Yet for the artist, variation for the sake of variation is meaningless; it must be contained in form to move from exercise to piece.

"Whoops! Johnny" is the young child's beginning etude on variation.

YES, PAPA

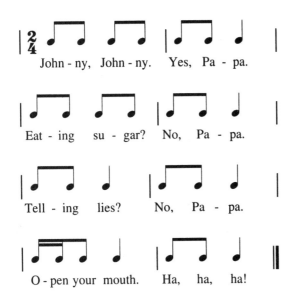

John - ny, John - ny. Yes, Pa - pa.

Eat - ing su - gar? No, Pa - pa.

Tell - ing lies? No, Pa - pa.

O - pen your mouth. Ha, ha, ha!

Music focus: Call and response

Language focus: Text interpretation

Activities:

• Students say *Yes, Papa* when teacher shakes head yes; *No, Papa*, when teacher shakes head no; and *Ha ha ha* when teacher points to open mouth. Teacher speaks first half of poem while miming actions—students respond.

• Half of the group recites the call, the other half, the response. Decide who says *Ha ha ha* (See Comments).

• Each group decides on a dramatic interpretation—is Papa stern or gentle? Is Johnny timid or sassy? Enact poem.

Variations:

• Experiment with other sets of opposites.

• Transfer the rhythm of "Yes, Papa" to body percussion, unpitched or pitched percussion.

Classroom Extensions:

• Have the students write a story about Johnny that highlights their interpretation of the text.

Comments:

I found "Yes, Papa" in a charming book by Francelia Butler entitled *Skipping Around the World*, where it was listed as an English rhyme from Kenya. This deceptively simple poem has deep interpretative possibilities. Ask the children the following questions (and share with you some of their answers):

Who is laughing? Johnny. *Why?* Because he was eating sugar and he got caught.
Why else could he be laughing? Because he <u>wasn't</u> eating sugar. *Why else?* Because he was eating it, but then he swallowed it or hid it under his tongue and tricked his father.
Who else could be laughing? His Papa. *Why?* Because he caught Johnny telling a lie.
Why else? Because he found out Johnny was telling the truth. *Who else could be laughing?* Both of them.
Why? Because Papa was eating sugar! And so on.

Because poems, stories, musical compositions, paintings and so on invite more than one interpretation, they provide a balance to academic emphasis on "the correct answer." Now that educators are talking about "critical thinking skills" and "higher level learning," it's time to put solid foundations under these castles in the air and nurture the capacity for symbol, metaphor and diverse interpretation. "Yes, Papa" might be thought of as a six-year-old's introduction to James Joyce's *Ulysses*.

JOHNNY WORKS WITH ONE HAMMER

John - ny works with one ham - mer, one ham - mer, one ham - mer.

John - ny works with one ham - mer, now he works with two.

Johnny works with two hammers . . . (Continue until five)

Johnny works with five hammers, five hammers, five hammers
Now he goes to sleep.

Music focus: Additive sequence
                    Steady beat
                    Rhythmic coordination

Language focus: Additive sequence

Activities:

• Teach in the traditional manner; mime hammering in the air with one hand for first verse, two for second, add tapping one foot for third, other for fourth, and nodding head for fifth, miming sleep at the end. All limbs express the beat in unison.

"Johnny works with five hammers"

"Now he goes to sleep."

Variations:

• Perform motions silently while audiating text.

• Express an ostinato rhythm with each body part.

e.g.:

• Perform a different rhythm with each limb (very challenging!).

e.g.:

• Perform with five different body parts (pinky, thumb, elbow, hip, nose).

• Divide group into five parts, each with a different percussion instrument (drum, shaker, scraper, woodblock, bell). Each plays steady beat in turn, adding parts as in the original game.

• As above, with movement, each group creating its own movement.

• One person at a time transfer the text to the drum set: right hand on ride cymbal, left on snare drum, right foot on bass drum, left foot on hi-hat, head vocalize the beat.

• As above, with ostinati variation.

Classroom Extensions:
• Compare this additive form to stories in which the numbers increase; e.g., *The Gingerbread Boy, The Golden Goose* . . .

Comments:
I include this well known song in our "Johnny" medley primarily for its exciting variations. It provides yet another example of how to turn a simple childhood game into a challenging exercise. It develops limb coordination (a necessary skill for playing the organ and drum set) and reminds us that rhythm can be expressed with the whole body.

WEE WILLIE WINKIE

Wee Willie Winkie runs through the town
Upstairs and downstairs in his nightgown.
Rapping at the window, crying through the lock
Are the children in their bed? For it's 8 o'clock.

"Rapping at the window,"

"Are the children in their bed?"

Music focus: Laban efforts*

Language focus: Expressive speech

Activities:

• Review list of opposites from previous activities. Brainstorm possibilities for each phrase and express freely (no obvious steady beat) with gestures. For example:

Wee Willie Winkie— high (flick—see comments)
runs through the town— fast (glide)
Upstairs and downstairs— high and low (float)
in his nightgown— whisper (dab)
Rapping at the window— strong (punch)
crying through the lock— whiny (wring)
Are the children in their bed?— forced smile (press)
For it's 8 o'clock— firm (slash)

Variations:

• Perform as above with gestures only.

• Small groups create their own interpretations.

• Accompany each movement with a different instrument, choosing those best suited to the quality.

Examples: high—high pitched woodblock; fast—glissando on xylophone; high and low—slide whistle; whisper—hand drum gently tapped with fingers; strong—snare drum played with drumstick; whiny—ratchet; forced smile—guiro slowly scraped; firm—large cymbal

Classroom Extensions:

• Read other poems from the language arts curriculum choosing different expressions according to text.

Comments:

I've often used this poem to accompany a short study in Laban efforts. The efforts are part of the ground-breaking movement work Rudolph Laban did in the first half of this century.* An in-depth study can take up to two years; for my purposes, I've used these ideas to support work with opposite qualities. The efforts represent eight archetypal movements of contrasting quality; punch, slash, glide, float, wring, press, dab and flick. "Wee Willie Winkie" offers a language base from which to explore these qualities; adding instruments makes another connection between the basic qualities of sound, movement and instrumental expression.

* Laban's remarkable career began with choreographing ballets before the first World War and soon extended into experiments that led to expressionism in modern dance. During World War II, he worked with factory workers in England to study problems of efficiency and stress in movement. As a teacher and theorist, he was concerned with exploring the range of movements between tension and relaxation (from which came the Laban efforts), matching movement to body types and notating movement in a system that came to be known as Labanotation.

SECOND STORY WINDOW

. . . and threw it out the window, the window, the second story window.
Think of a rhyme, say it on time and throw it out the window.

Music focus: Phrase structure

Language focus: Comprehension

Activity:

• Teacher requests a nursery rhyme from the group. All recite, replacing the last line with *. . . and threw it out the window . . .* as in the following example:

Hickory dickory dock, the mouse ran up the clock,
The clock struck one, the mouse ran down and
threw it out the window, the window, the second story window.
Think of a rhyme, say it on time and throw it out the window.

This refrain can also be sung, often as follows:

• Groups of two to six people think of a rhyme and change it as shown above. Each group then recites its altered rhyme in turn, with all joining in on the refrain. However, no group may repeat another group's rhyme. If group C chose "Hickory Dickory Dock" and group A recites it, group C has to quickly think and find another—on time— before their turn (talking permitted while another group is performing). After all the groups have shared their rhyme, group A continues with a new one. If a group repeats a rhyme or fails to think of one on time, it goes "out" (the window?). (The teacher may secretly write the title of each rhyme recited to keep track and judge fairly.) Play until only one group remains.

Variations:

• In a circle, recite rhymes individually in turn.

Classroom Extensions:

• Discuss the new meaning of the rhymes with their changed endings. Do they make sense? Look for rhymes that don't work.

Comments:

I learned this game at a family camp in the Sierra Mountains of California. It was a wonderful experience except for the limited repertoire of the teenage counselors - 55 renditions of *Bingo* everyday! But they compensated for the *Bingo* torture by introducing me to this fun game. It is now a standard in both my classroom and my workshops—a great way to determine the nursery rhyme repertoire of a particular group. In my adult classes, I've never had a group go out (after fifteen minutes I stop the game!). However, it's a different story with kids, confirming my sense that nursery rhymes are an endangered species.

The eerie thing about this game is how consistently the tacked-on ending makes sense in so many rhymes. "Jack Sprat," "Jack and Jill," "Humpty Dumpty," "Little Miss Muffet," "Peter, Peter Pumpkin Eater," "Old Mother Hubbard" without exception are throwing someone, something or being thrown out the window! (Remember this game on long car rides or parties when people tire of charades.)

SECOND STORY WINDOW – WITH DRUMS

Music focus: Rubato phrasing

Movement improvisation

Language focus: Comprehension

Activities:

• Recite the rhymes presented in the "Second Story Window" game in a free rubato fashion.

• Use hand drums as props for spontaneously enacting the text. The drum can be Jack Sprat's bowl, Humpty Dumpty's belly, Jack and Jill's pail of water, Doctor Foster's umbrella, the sun Sally goes around, the candlestick Jack jumps over; it can play the galloping hoofbeats of the Farmer's gray mare, Miss Muffet's shout when she sees the spider, the clock striking one and more. Naturally, it can also play the underlying beats or fill in the rests.

| "Doctor Foster went to Gloucester" | "Jack jumped over the candlestick" | "Rub a dub dub, three men in a tub" |

Variations:

• Have children create their own versions of a rhyme with drums, alone or as a group.

• As above, using different instruments or objects—scarves, paper plates, and so on.

Classroom Extensions:

• Create dramatizations of these rhymes from the above improvisations using props.

Comments:

Although we usually say these rhymes with a steady beat, it is equally important to speak them freely. In this case, pausing between lines gives space to respond with the improvised action. Repeating the rhyme and drawing from the children's ideas, the initial improvisations can begin to form into set dramatizations.

This activity cultivates the child's natural talent—transforming objects through play. Montessori, Steiner, Piaget and other great educational philosophers recognize these activities as the foundation of later symbol-making and metaphorical ability. By engaging each object with their imagination, children learn in concrete terms what they will later need to understand in abstract terms—that each thing can stand for something else. The connection between Jack Sprat's hand drum bowl and algebraic variables may not seem immediately obvious, but it indeed exists. Knowing this helps us all to understand the importance of the arts to the child's total development.

Such long-range thinking is the province of the adult. Meanwhile, the child is thrilled in the moment to be given permission to do what comes naturally—fantasy play. Acting out these rhymes can happen in either the music or language class, bringing them alive in a way that brightens both classrooms.

SECOND STORY WINDOW – WITH OPPOSITE CARDS

Music focus: Composition

Choreography

Language focus: Antonyms

Activities:

• Brainstorm a list of opposites with the class and write each pair on a file card. Post the list of nursery rhymes generated from the "Second Story Window" game. Form groups of two to eight people (larger groups work better).

• Each group draws a card and chooses a nursery rhyme to perform using the opposite qualities listed on the card. The choice of rhyme may be inspired by the card ("Jack Sprat" for fat/thin, "Humpty Dumpty" for clumsy/graceful, "Jack and Jill" for high/low;) but needn't be directly related to the opposites. Some inspired adult performances have come from such opposites as heaven/hell, caffeinated/decaffeinated, Republican/Democrat! Set a time limit for preparing the rhyme—use all available media.

• Groups perform one at a time.

Variations:

• To create a rondo form, all recite or sing *threw it out the window, the window, the second story window. Think of a rhyme, say it on time and throw it out the window* between each performance.

Classroom extensions:

• Play an antonym word association game; one person says a word and the next responds with its antonym. This could be played with or without a steady beat, with people going "out" if they miss the answer.

• Discuss the difference between opposite and different; e.g. is there an opposite for apple? For book? For cat?

• Use the dramatization of opposites as an opportunity for discussion of stereotypes and archetypes (at the appropriate level!). How did the students portray man and woman? Smart and stupid?

Comments:

This structure gives a lot of room to the group imagination and yet provides a firm anchor (the opposite cards) for inspiration. The interplay of various media, attention to text, built-in contrast, inevitable humor and organic forms results in performances that make the usual rhythmic work we do with rhymes seem mundane! This is a good "final exam" for the various opposite exercises. Consider refining some performances for use in a larger show, or as part of a larger story.

LUCY LOCKET

Lucy Locket lost her pocket, Kitty Fisher found it
There was not a penny in it, but a ribbon 'round it.

Music focus: Dynamics (Forte/piano)
Quarter/eighth notes

Activities:

• Children recite rhyme with eyes closed while teacher hides an object (I use a piece of cloth to represent the "pocket"). After singing the song, they open their eyes and try to find Lucy's pocket. (You may wish to set parameters—places off limits for looking, rules about running and so on.) Teacher plays a drum while the children search, playing loudly when someone is close to the hidden object and softly when they're far away. The child who finds the "pocket" hides it the next time.

Variations:

• Use this melody:

• If the hider needs more time, lengthen the text as follows:
Kitty Fisher found it, Kitty Fisher found it,
There was not a penny in it, but a ribbon 'round it.

• Discover which words have a contrasting rhythm to the text that precedes it (*Lucy Locket . . .* and *found it, There was not a . . .* and *'round it.*).

• Name the note values (quarter, eighth) and explore the following variations following the rhythm of the text (each person can perform a pair of variations—pat/clap, jog/walk— or half the group can do one while the other half does the other):

Eighth notes—pat on knees, jog, move in one body part, speak in one type of voice, sing on one note, play on drum, express in percussive vocal sound.

Quarter notes—clap, walk, move in another body part, speak with a different voice, sing on another note, play on bell, express in different percussive vocal sound.

• Notate the text:

Comments:

This is a favorite game of the little ones. It's always amusing to watch how the three-year-old "hider" gives away the location of the hidden object—often by pointing right to it! The drum playing helps shift that to another level. It also is fascinating to watch how all the searchers go immediately to the spot where the pocket was last hidden!

This rhyme is one of several offered here that introduces contrasting eighth and quarter notes (see also "Whoops! Johnny," "Peter Peter Pumpkin Eater," "Bate Bate Chocolate"). Once we identify these contrasts, we can re-enter the world of open-ended process that we explored with "Whoops! Johnny." This approach creates a class atmosphere of surprise and delight that simultaneously anchors musical experience in the whole body, voice and imagination.

TWO LITTLE BLACKBIRDS

Music focus: Hocket

Musical structure

Language focus: Rhyming

Activities:

• Teach rhyme and ask children to enact it with their hands, one for Jack, one for Jill.

• Divide class into four groups. All recite first two lines; each group recites one part from the last two lines as follows:

Fly away	*Come back*	*Jack*	*Jill*
Group a	Group b	Group c	Group d

• Transfer to selected unpitched percussion.

e.g.: hand drum	guiro	cowbell	woodblock
Group a	Group b	Group c	Group d

• Create an abstract notation of the last two phrases.

	Group	or	Group
e.g.:	a b a c		✌ ✏ ✌ ☎
	d b d c		☆ ✏ ☆ ☎

Variations:

• Enact rhyme using entire body; half the class as Jack, half as Jill.

• Transfer selected phrases to melodic instruments—xylophones, recorders, voice—to create melodic phrases.

• Create a new piece based on the abstract score—new phrases or rhythms for each section.
   e.g.:

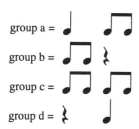

Classroom Extensions:

• Create a new poem based on the rhyming structure. Maintain alliteration in the names.
   e.g.: *Two little blackbirds sitting on the wall.*
   One named Peter and the other named Paul . . .

   Two little blackbirds sitting on the rug.
   One named Donna and the other named Doug . . .

Comments:

The interest in this poem lies in its unique phrase structure. The recurrence of *Jack* and *Jill*, preceded by a different phrase each time, is refreshing to hear after so many simpler forms.

ROSES ARE RED

Ros - es are red, Vio - lets are blue. Su - gar is sweet, And so are you!

Music focus: Rests

Phrase length and contrast

Language focus: Love poems

Activities:

• Leader plays the rhythm of the first three phrases on the high bell, and plays the last phrase; *and so are you!* on a low bell. Following the leader, all walk to the beat of the high bell and jump with the last three strokes on the low bell. Continue until a circle is formed. All sit and join the leader's rhythm, clapping the high bell part and patting the low bell part on the floor.

• Students try to guess the rhyme from the rhythm played. Check all answers by reciting them with the pattern.

• All learn poem echo fashion, recite and snap "empty" beats (rests).

• Teacher plays snaps on a hotel desk bell, then passes it around the circle (while reciting). Each child rings bell at the end of a phrase without losing the beat.

• Put bell on a stool in the center of the circle; each steps in and rings in turn as above.

• As above, but with bell on floor, tap with foot.

• All stand facing a partner. Recite first three lines while walking on the beat away from partner, run back at the beginning of the fourth phrase and join hands on the word *you.*

• As above, but begin back to back; no turning to find partner until the last phrase—then proceed as above (end facing partner holding hands).

• Play as above. Partners not returning in time are "out"; they play on instruments for the next game—woodblock for rhythm of first three phrases, drum for the last phrase, triangle for the rests (instruments are arranged in a row at the edge of the space). Each person out chooses one of the above to play. Continue the game until one set of partners remains.

Variations:

• When only a few partners remain, change to running to a new partner each time.

Classroom Extensions:

• Investigate other examples of the most popular theme in Western poetry— love!

Comments:

This rhyme is an essential part of a teacher's Valentine's Day repertoire and the activity, a wonderful "win/win" game. It's fascinating to watch the children decide whether they're happy or sad when they go "out" because those who are itching to play the instruments have to struggle against their desire to "win"!

PIN MARIN

Pin marin de Don pingue
Cacara, macara, pipiri fue
A - E - I-O-U
El burro sabe mas que tu

Phonetic Pronunciation:

Peen mah reen day dohn peen-gway

Cah-cah-rah, mah-cah-rah, pee-pee-ree fway

ah-ay-ee-oh-oo

Ehl boo-roh sah-bay mahss kay too

Translation: Nonsense words except for last line: *The donkey knows more than you.*

Music focus: Layered ostinati
Melodic invention

Language focus: Spanish vowels
Poetry performance

Activities:

• Teach poem echo fashion, one phrase at a time.

• Create ostinati from the text; one group speaks each of the following ostinati in turn while another recites the complete rhyme:

| 1 | A | E | I | O | U | * |

| 2 | Ca - ca - ra ma - ca - ra, | Ca - ca - ra ma - ca - ra |

| 3 | bu - rro, El | bu - rro, El |

| 4 | sa - be mas que | tú * * * |

• Transfer above to body percussion, one group per pattern and a fifth speaking the text:
1) pat floor 2) pat knees 3) clap and rub hands 4) clap words, snap on the rests (* *).

40

• Transfer to unpitched percussion as above: 1) hand drums 2) agogo bell 3) guiro or shaker 4) double woodblock. Text can be spoken or played on snare drum over the layered parts. Here is the notated version:

Variations:

• Speak or play text in canon over supporting ostinati.

• Create a melody for text by choosing a scale, creating a first phrase, repeating it three times and creating a finishing phrase. Here is an example in C pentatonic:

• Create accompanying drone on the bass xylophone (use notes C and G).

• Create a form for performance, as follows:

> Layer vocal ostinati one at a time. When all have entered, speak text while ostinati continues. (2x)
> Play ostinati on percussion, sing melody (2x), layering and entering as above.
> Play melody on xylophone with supporting drone and percussion ostinati. (2x)
> Percussion "break"— percussion soloist improvises over ostinati. (Equivalent of 2x)
> Tutti: Play, sing and continue ostinati. (2x)

Classroom Extensions:
- Compare the English long vowel sounds—A-E-I-O-U— with the Spanish pronunciation (AH-AY-EE-OH-OO).

- Apply the idea presented here (extracting and repeating portions of text while reciting whole text) to another poem.

Comments:

I found this rhyme in Virginia Ebinger's fine book *Ninez: Spanish Songs, Games and Stories of Childhood*. I first taught it in Finland as a neutral language poem— neither English nor Finnish. Its nonsense text in another language freed us from cultural stylistic assumptions and allowed us to simply explore its rhythmic and melodic possibilities.

Here we begin to enter the work of moving these rhymes toward full orchestrations, starting with the ostinato, a universal musical device used extensively in the Orff-Schulwerk. The ostinato (plural ostinati) is a simple repeated rhythmic or melodic pattern. Its elemental musical quality and easy accessibility make it an ideal device for work with children.

This rhyme shows how ostinati can be derived directly from a text to accompany that text. Although ostinati should *complement* the rhythm of the rhyme, this approach works if there are enough ostinati to mask the parallel rhythms. (For example, if A-E-I-O-U is the only ostinato, there will be a strong parallel rhythm when the text arrives at A-E-I-O-U. If, as in this case, that ostinato is one of four, that parallel will pass unnoticed.) Three other devices for avoiding parallels are used here: dividing the rhythm between two tones (ca-cara, ma-cara— ♪ ♫ ♪ ♫); altering the rhythm (el burrr-o); displacing the rhythm (sabe mas que tu).

Here we have also taken our first step toward melodic and harmonic development.

BATE BATE CHOCOLATE

Phonetic Pronunciation:

Oon-dohs-trays-tchoh

" " " coh

" " " lah

" " " tay

Bah-tay, bah-tay-tchoh-coh-lah-tay

Cohn ah-rohss ee cohn toh-mah-tay

Translation: *1-2-3- cho, 1-2-3-co, 1-2-3-la, 1-2-3- te (the syllables of the word cho-co-la-te)*
Beat, beat the chocolate, with rice and tomatoes

Musical focus: Quarter/eighth notes
Diminishing phrases

Language focus: Syllables
Dividing text for "Reader's Theater"

Activities:

• Write text on board as above (indicate plain and boldface with colored chalk or markers). Leader recites words in plain text, group responds with text in bold.

• One group recites all the words in plain text, a second group recites the words in bold and both together the underlined words.

• As above, clapping text while audiating words.

• As above, transfer to unpitched percussion.

Variations:
• Divide up the phrases as follows:

Bate, bate, chocolate, con arroz y con tomate

Bate, bate, chocolate, con arroz y con **tomate**

Bate, bate, chocolate, con arroz y **con tomate**

Bate, bate, chocolate, con arroz y **con tomate**

Bate, bate, chocolate, con **arroz y con tomate**

Bate, bate, chocolate, **con arroz y con tomate**

Bate, bate, **chocolate, con arroz y con tomate**

Bate, **bate, chocolate, con arroz y con tomate**

Bate, bate, chocolate, con arroz y con tomate

• Speak the plain italic, audiating the bold italic of each phrase. Reverse.

• One group speaks the plain italic, the other, the bold.

Classroom Extensions:
• Apply this device (dividing up the lines amongst readers in phrases of different lengths) to another poem.

• Note the difference in difficulty between text and music (see Comments).

Comments:
This rhyme from Mexico is about making chicken mole (chocolate with rice and tomatoes). It is traditionally chanted while counting fingers on the first part and rubbing hands together on the second to mime beating chocolate with a *molinillo*, a carved wooden beater that grinds the wedges of Mexican chocolate.

"Bate Chocolate" highlights the contrast between quarter and eighth notes. I changed the first part from "uno-dos-tres" to "un-dos-tres" for a musical reason—to make it all quarter notes—and was thrilled when a Spanish friend told me that it was actually common to count like that in Spain! The second part of the text gives us two syllables per beat (all eighth notes!) making "Bate Chocolate" a pedagogical delight—an authentic rhyme that serves the music teacher's conceptual goals. It also makes for some exciting music, with the steady rhythmic flow building with a crescendo and ending on an upbeat. This is an example of how we can be enriched by going beyond our English inheritance of rhyme—it is rare to find an authentic Mother Goose rhyme with all quarter or all eighth notes!

"Bate Chocolate" helps show us the difference between rhythm in music and rhythm in language. Speaking the division con ar**roz y** con to**mate** is much more difficult than clapping the same because of the way the words are divided. The variation offered moves with the word rather than the beat and makes for a different kind of challenge.

TANTOS RIOS

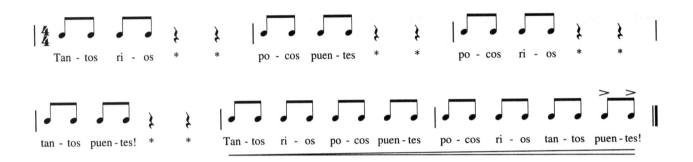

Phonetic Pronunciation:

Tahn-tohs ree-ohs poh-cohs pwen-tays

Poh-cohs ree-ohs tahn-tohss pwen-tays

Translation: *So many rivers, so few bridges*
So few rivers, so many bridges

Musical focus: Canon

Quarter/eighth notes

Language focus: Nouns/adjectives

Activities:

• Speak text with two claps (indicated by an asterisk) between each phrase. Speak the last line in crescendo, clapping only on the final *puentes.*

• Transfer text to body percussion, i.e., step or pat the text.

• Perform in two part canon (enter after *rios*)—speaking only; body percussion only; speaking and body percussion together.

• Perform in four part canon, entering after *tantos.*

Variations:

• Four groups, one word per group. Perform (speaking and/or body percussion) in the order given with everyone clapping on asterisks and final *puentes.*

rios

tantos   *pocos*

puentes

Classroom Extensions:

• Small groups create new text in Spanish and act it out for others to guess. For example:
Tantos hombres, poco tiempo, tanto tiempo, pocos hombres.

Comments:

This rhyme comes from a delightful book of Spanish *trabalenguas* (tongue twisters) that I found in Oaxaca, Mexico (*No Me Maravillaria Yo*- Luz Maria Chapela/ Liliana Felipe). It is yet another example of a Spanish rhyme with a steady flow of eighth notes (see also, "Bate Bate"). I have added the quarter note claps to extend the rhyme and provide contrast. This score is primarily for voice and body percussion and like the others, easily transferable to movement, percussion and barred instruments.

The structure of "Tantos Rios"—abcd cbad—is akin to that of "Two Little Blackbirds." The variation brings out this unique feature, while the classroom extension invites creativity on all levels— new text, dramatic/movement enactment and guessing by the audience. Your class might want to create a small collection of new rhymes in this form.

MAN IN CAR

Man in car, went to bar. Feel-ing nif-ty, do-ing fif-ty. Hit a pole, poor old soul. Doc-tor's fee, cem-e-tery.*

* See comments.

Musical focus: Hocket/Orchestration

Language focus: Grammatical analysis

Activities:

- Write poem on board. Identify all nouns and underline them. Then with verbs as one group, adjectives as another, and prepositions and articles as a fourth, identify each group with a distinctive marking, as in the following example:

> <u>Man</u> *in* <u>car</u>,
>
> **Went** *to* <u>bar</u>.
>
> **Feeling** nifty,
>
> **Doing** fifty.
>
> **Hit** *a* <u>pole</u>,
>
> Poor old <u>soul</u>.
>
> Doctor's <u>fee</u>,
>
> ***<u>Cemetery</u>.*** (All say last word)

- Each person picks a part of speech and only speaks, sings, gestures, moves or plays an instrument on the corresponding words. Students decide which instruments will accompany each part of speech (drums—nouns, whistles—verbs, etc.) and create a form for the final piece. For example, one group could speak while another moves, then all pick up instruments and play while another group enacts the story, and so on.

Variations:

- As above with melodic instruments playing set tones for each part of speech.

Classroom Extensions:

- Apply above approach to other rhymes and poems.

Comments:

This rhyme from Australia is a lesson in grammar, a springboard to composition and a part of the health and safety curriculum. I found it in Francelia Butler's book, *Skipping Around the World.* This simple idea of making grammar audible offers yet another mode for the language class to experience parts of speech and gives the music class an unorthodox approach to composition.

I used "Man in Car" in one of my workshops and learned a valuable lesson about the problems of transferring oral tradition to print. We were all bothered by the odd rhythm of the word *cemetery* and as we were trying to find a way to make it fit, a participant who was, amazingly enough, from Australia, said, *"No, no, it's not cem-e-ter-y, it's cem-e-tr'y!"* (pronounced *ce-me tree*).

IF ALL THE SEAS

If all the seas were one sea, what a <u>great</u> sea that would be! If all the trees were one tree, what a great tree that would be! If all the ax - es were one ax, what a <u>great</u> ax that would be! If all the men were one man, what a <u>great</u> man that would be! If the <u>great</u> man took the <u>great</u> axe and cut down the <u>great</u> tree, let it fall in - to the <u>great</u> sea, what a splish-splash that would be!

Music focus: Rhythmic accent

Language focus: Accent and meaning

  Plurals

Activities:

• Recite the poem as written, with accents on *<u>great</u>*.

• Decide on rhythmic interpretation, for example:

• Accent different words, e.g. *seas, trees, axes, men* and their singular form, *one* and *that, if* and *what* . . .

• Transfer to hand drums and practice accenting chosen words.

Variations:

• Perform all chosen accents simultaneously (one person or more per part).

Classroom Extensions:

• Study the variety of plurals and singulars—*seas/sea, trees/tree, axes/ax, men/man.*
Substitute other nouns, with attention to sense and unusual plurals and singulars. For example: *houses/house, mice/mouse, mouths/mouth, teeth/tooth.* (Last section: *If that great tooth in that great mouth in the great mouse chewed the great house, what a problem that would be!*)

• Discuss the difference in meaning when different words are accented.

Comments:

Both music and language begin in the ear and both equally share some difficulties in trying to capture sound in print. The quality of *accent*—giving greater emphasis to particular words or sounds—is indicated in music by a mark over the given note $>$, in language through the use of *italic*, underline, **boldface** or combination of ___*all three!*___ Whole phrases can be given emphasis in music with the dynamic marking of *Forte*, in language through the exclamation point! Here again, music and language share these characteristics, but each also has its distinct quality. Shifting the accent in music changes the feeling of the rhythmic phrase— ♪♪♪ in contrast to ♪♪♪ . Shifting the accent in language can change the *meaning* of the phrase. I once heard the poet Robert Bly lead an audience in reciting a line of poetry from the thirteenth century poet Rumi: *Let the beauty we love be what we do.* As the audience accented each separate word—*do, we, what, be, love, beauty*—the meaning of the line shifted noticeably.

PEASE PORRIDGE HOT

Music Focus: Rhythmic elements—beat, duration values, rest, downbeat, phrase
Hocket

Language Focus: Related literature

Activities:

• Pat beat on knees while reciting text.

• Pat pulse (two pats per beat) on knees with alternating hands while reciting text.

• Perform a four beat pattern while reciting text, e.g.: floor-knees-clap-snap. Strike floor on the first word of each phrase; internalize last three motions.

• Recite text, snap "empty" beats after *hot, cold* and *old.*

• Clap rhythm of words on the first three lines, pat chest on *Nine days old.*

• Clap with flat hands on rhyming words *hot, pot.*

• Clap with cupped hands on rhyming words *cold, old.*

• Perform all seven parts above simultaneously (one person or more per part).

• As above, text unspoken.

• Transfer each part to unpitched percussion and/or movement.

• Create a score from the text by highlighting each part; divide group and perform.

Pease porridge <u>hot</u> 𝄾
Pease porridge (cold) 𝄾
Pease porridge in the <u>pot</u>
Nine days (old). 𝄾

Some like it <u>hot</u> 𝄾
Some like it (cold) 𝄾
Some like it in the <u>pot</u>
Nine days (old). 𝄾

Variations:

• Create an abstraction of the score.

☆	✌	✌	⇨	✿
☆	✌	✌	✎	✿
☆	✌	✌	✈ ☎ ⇨	
☆	✌		✎	✿

Π	ρ	ρ	η	*
Π	ρ	ρ	o	*
Π	ρ	ρ	ι τ	η
Π	*ρ*		*o*	*

• Individuals express as many rhythmic components as possible; for example:
Tap beat with right foot, stamp downbeat with left, pat rhythm on knee, pat other hand on chest for rhyming words, click tongue for rests ("empty" beats).

Classroom Extensions:

• The class makes a list of all poems, stories, movies, songs and rhymes that include or refer to any of the words in the poem, e.g., the poem "Father William," the story "Goldilocks and the Three Bears," the song "Hot Cross Buns," the movie "Some Like It Hot," and the rhyme "Some Flew East."

Comments:

"Pease Porridge Hot" again uses the hocketing principle to create a unique arrangement. The main interest lies in the surprise of the third line, with no rest and the rhyming word falling on beat 4 instead of 3.

This arrangement offers a review of the basic rhythmic concepts explored throughout this book. The last variation is a challenge for even the most accomplished musician!

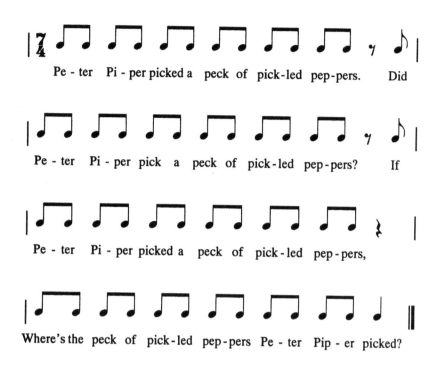

Pe - ter Pi - per picked a peck of pick-led pep-pers. Did

Pe - ter Pi - per pick a peck of pick-led pep-pers? If

Pe - ter Pi - per picked a peck of pick-led pep-pers,

Where's the peck of pick-led pep-pers Pe - ter Pip - er picked?

Music focus: 7/4 meter

Language focus: Alliteration

Verb conjugation

Activities:

• Memorize rhyme; groups experiment with different meters and phrasing and share results.

• Choose a meter for entire group to try—example in 7/4:

7/4	Peter Piper picked a peck of pickled peppers. Did	Peter Piper pick a peck of pickled peppers? If
	pat clap pat clap pat clap clap	pat clap pat clap pat clap clap

	Peter Piper picked a peck of pickled peppers.	Where's the peck of pickled peppers Peter Piper picked?
	pat clap pat clap pat clap clap	pat clap pat clap pat clap clap

Variations:

• Perform rhyme with body percussion in two-part canon. Experiment with different entrances.

• Perform in a different meter, adding or subtracting words. My third grade class created a 4/4 version by adding the word *purple* to the first three lines (the last line stayed the same with a rest at the end): *Peter Piper picked a peck of / pickled purple peppers* . . . (keep *Did* and *If* as upbeats). Another group created a 3/4 version by deleting *pickled*: *Peter Piper picked a / peck of peppers* . . . For 5/4, delete *peck* and *of* and make *pepper* singular: *Peter Piper picked a / pepper* . . .

Classroom Extensions:

• Create a rhyme with a different alliteration phoneme using the rhyme's structure:*
  Tommy Turtle told Tall Tales to a tortoise.
  Did Tommy Turtle tell Tall Tales to a tortoise?
  If Tommy Turtle told Tall Tales to a tortoise,
  Which Tall Tales to a tortoise had Tommy Turtle told?

• Play spoken parts on unpitched percussion instruments that evoke the starting sound of the new rhyme—woodblocks for "p," shakers for "s," cowbells for "c" and so on.

Comments:

The 7/4 implied phrasing is a refreshing change from the 4s and 8s of most English rhymes. Those of us exposed mostly to 2/4, 4/4, 3/4 and 6/8 meter and trained to approach meter through counting find odd meters (5/4, 7/8 etc.) a frightening experience. Yet children approaching meter through language and movement have no such problem.

The verb conjugation in line 2 makes this a good crossover language arts lesson.

* For an entire alphabet of rhymes based on "Peter Piper," see Iona and Peter Opie's *A Nursery Companion.*

PETER PETER PUMPKIN EATER

Peter Peter Pumpkin Eater
Had a wife and couldn't keep her.
Put her in a pumpkin shell and
There he kept her very well.

Musical focus: Eighth notes
Hocket
Polymetric accent

Language focus: Text interpretation

Activities:

Percussionist Keith Terry's approach to body percussion adds a new dimension to the snap, claps, pats and stamps of traditional Orff practice.* His idea of sounding rhythmic phrases on the body in groups of 3, 5, 7 and 9 stroke patterns is an ingenious way of teaching complex patterns. Leading with the dominant clapping hand and flowing smoothly down the body, the four patterns are:

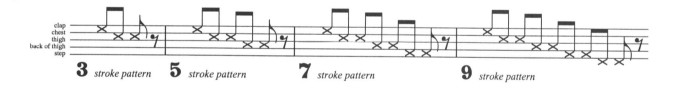

3 *stroke pattern*   **5** *stroke pattern*   **7** *stroke pattern*   **9** *stroke pattern*

• Teach the patterns one at a time until group is comfortable.

* Keith's work in both body percussion and percussion can be heard on his CD *Crosspulse.*

• Recite rhyme with the 3 stroke pattern; an eighth note rest between each cycle is indicated by an asterisk.

Pe-ter Pe-ter Pump-kin Ea-ter Had a   wife and could-n't   keep her. (etc.)

cl- ch- ch *   cl-   ch- ch- * cl-   ch- ch- *   cl- ch- ch   *

• Recite with the 5 stroke accompaniment (ends on clap).

Pe-ter   Pe-ter Pump-kin Ea- ter Had a wife and could-n't keep her. Put her (etc.)

cl- ch-   ch- th- th-   * cl- ch-   ch- th- th- *   cl- ch- ch- th   th   *

• Recite with the 7 stroke accompaniment (ends on back of thigh).

Pe- ter Pe- ter Pump-kin Ea- ter Had a   wife and could-n't keep her. (etc.)

cl- ch- ch- th-   th- bk- bk *   cl- ch- ch- th-   th- bk- bk- *

• Recite with the 9 stroke accompaniment (ends on clap).

Pe- ter Pe-ter Pump-kin Ea- ter Had a wife and could-n't keep her. Put her in a (etc.)

 cl- ch- ch- th- th-   bk- bk- st- st- * cl- ch- ch- th- th- bk- bk- st- st-*

• Divide group in four, one accompanying pattern per group.

• Repeat above process without rests.

i.e: The 3 stroke pattern

>   *Pe-ter Pe-ter Pump-kin Ea-ter Had a wife and could-n't keep her. (etc.)*
>
>   cl -ch- ch-cl-   ch- ch- cl- ch- ch- cl- ch- ch- cl- ch-   ch- cl

The 7 stroke pattern ends with three claps on text *very well.*

The 9 stroke pattern ends with a 3 and a clap on text *her very well*

• Divide into eight groups, each group speaking only the syllables that coincide with claps. Half of the groups with eighth note rests, half without.

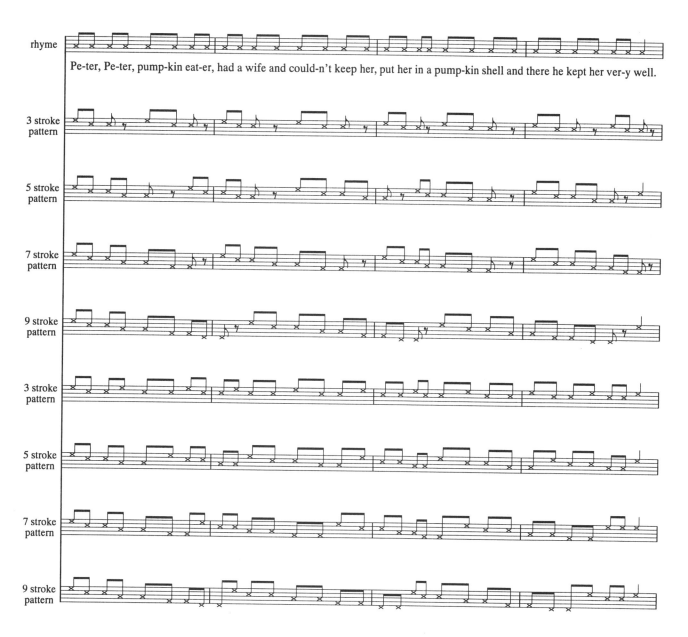

Variations:

• Any combination of the eight patterns above.

Classroom Extensions:

• Discuss the meaning of the text and the history of husband/wife relations. Compare to the second verse below and discuss the connection between literacy and love.

Peter, Peter, pumpkin eater

Had another, and didn't love her;

Peter learned to read and spell,

And then he loved her very well.

Comments:

In spite of a high degree of feminist consciousness, this politically incorrect rhyme was the hit of my 1996 Orff Teacher Training class, appearing time and again as the chosen poem in the homework assignments! Perhaps the students were attracted to the constant flow of eighth notes building energetically to the climax of the final *well*.

The above arrangement was inspired by that class's enthusiasm for this rhyme and presents quite a challenge for musicians of all ages. If your kids complain about nursery rhymes being too babyish, smile and say, "Try this one."

GLOSSARY OF MUSICAL TERMS

Audiation—Also referred to as "inner hearing," this is a primary device for transferring concrete words to abstract rhythms—silently thinking the words while playing its rhythms.

Canon—Two or more groups performing the same piece beginning at different times (as in the classic "Row, Row, Row Your Boat"). In song, there are special considerations for entrances and melodies for the parts to fit—with speech, most anything can work.

Hocket—This term comes from a European compositional practice in the thirteenth century, but the principle is universal—dividing a piece in such a way that all players internalize its linear flow, but only sound specific notes in the sequence. European handbell choirs, Indonesian angklung groups, Peruvian panpipe players and some African xylophone traditions all use this technique. Hocketing is an ideal device for speech pieces as each child audiates the whole text, speaking only the pre-assigned words.

Meter—A word shared by poetry and music alike, with similarities but notable differences. Meter in language is colorfully defined by *iambs, trochees, spondees, dactyls* and *pyrrhics*, specific stress patterns of syllables within a *foot*, the language equivalent of music's *beat*. Each line is further defined by the number of *feet, pentameter* (five feet) being a classic English form. Meter in music shares these characteristics of stressed and unstressed sounds and number of beats in a measure, but uses its own mathematical vocabulary—6/8 (the natural meter of most nursery rhymes), 2/4, 3/4 and 4/4 the most common in Western music.

Ostinato—A short, repeated pattern, rhythmic or melodic, that supports a text. Complementary **ostinati** are two or more patterns that "fill in" each other's spaces.

DOUG GOODKIN

Doug Goodkin teaches music and movement to children between three years old and the eighth grade at The San Francisco School, where he has taught since 1975. He is an internationally recognized practitioner of Orff-Schulwerk, teaching Orff courses throughout North America, Europe and Australia. He is the director of the Mills College Orff Certification Course in Oakland, CA and teaches his own course on Jazz and Orff-Schulwerk through San Francisco State University.

Doug has published numerous articles on Orff in contemporary culture and is an author of the Macmillan/McGraw-Hill textbook series *Share the Music*. He is a founding member of the Orff-based adult performing group Xephyr. Doug is known for his innovative application of Orff-Schulwerk across various disciplines, particularly language arts, jazz, and multi-cultural music.

Bowmar's
ADVENTURES IN MUSIC LISTENING
An Integrated Elementary Listening Program
for Kindergarten through 8th Grade Classes
By Dr. Leon Burton, Dr. Charles Hoffer, Dr. William Hughes and June Hinckley

- **A fun, innovative approach to music listening for today's student**
- **Directly correlated with the National Standards in Music Education Goals 2000**
- **Easy-to-follow lesson plan format**
- **Active participation experiences for students in every lesson**

Selected pages from Big Book, Level 1

Includes great works by: Bizet, Debussy, Ravel, Tchaikovsky, Bach, Mozart, Verdi, Grieg and many others

Level 1, Grades K-2

The Teacher's Guide/CD — Level 1
(BMR08201) $49.95
contains lesson plans for each of the 32 musical selections, including:

- Anticipated Outcomes
- Historical Information
- Composer Information
- Musical Features Sketch
- Cross-Curricular Connections
- National Standards
- Full-length CD

The Big Book — Level 1
(BMR08201B) $49.95
contains magnificent full-color illustrations depicting each of the 32 pieces in the program

Student Activity Book — Level 1
(BMR08201S) $2.50
provides individual and group experiences that reinforce the learning in each lesson

Student Coloring Book — Level 1
(BMR08201C) $9.95
contains the Big Book illustrations re-created and ready for students' coloring activity (with our permission to photocopy)

Level 2, Grades 3-5

The Teacher's Guide/CD — Level 2
(BMR08202) $49.95
contains lesson plans for each of the 20 musical selections, including:

- Anticipated Outcomes
- Historical Information
- Composer Information
- Musical Features Sketch
- Cross-Curricular Connections
- National Standards
- Full-length CD

Student Activity Book — Level 2
(BMR08202S) $2.50
provides individual and group experiences that reinforce the learning in each lesson

Level 3, Grades 6-8, available soon

WE SALUTE THE
NATIONAL MUSIC STANDARDS

WARNER BROS. PUBLICATIONS
A Warner Music Group Company

Available at your local music store

YOUR SOURCE FOR ORFF

CRITTERS AND OTHER CREATURES

by Konnie Saliba
(BMR08005)

A fun collection of songs and poems for children by renowned educator Konnie Saliba (1996 recipient of the American Orff-Schulwerk Distinguished Service Award). Each of the 25 delightful songs focuses on reinforcing important musical elements and ideas. Teaching suggestions are provided along with many opportunities for creative choices.

5 SPIRITUALS FOR CHORUS

by Steven Calantropio
(with Orff Instrument Accompaniment)
(EL03969) Conductor's Score
(EL03969SB) Student Book

CELEBRATE!

by Alice Olsen
(BMR08003)
Sing and play about special days.

CONGA TOWN

by Jim Solomon
(BMR08002)
Percussion ensembles for upper elementary and middle school.

THE WORLD DANCE SERIES

CANADIAN FOLK DANCES
(BMR05119) Book and CD

FOLK DANCES FROM AROUND THE WORLD
(BMR05114) Book and CD

FOLK DANCES FROM FRANCE
(BMR05122) Book and CD

FOLK DANCES OF HAWAII
(BMR05116) Book and CD

FOLK DANCES OF LATIN AMERICA
(BMR05115) Book and CD

MEXICAN FOLK DANCES
(BMR05117) Book and CD

SING ME A SONG

by Konnie Saliba
(BMR08001)
A collection of songs and games for children.

TOPS IN POPS

by Marilyn Copeland Davidson
(BMR08004)
Oldies but goodies in simple arrangements.

TRADITIONAL SONGS OF SINGING CULTURES: A WORLD SAMPLER

by Dr. Patricia Shehan Campbell
(BMR05123CD) Book and CD
An Orff supplement, with traditional folk tunes from all over the world.

THE MUSIC OF PAUL WINTER — EARTH: VOICES OF A PLANET

This collaboration between Grammy-winning composer/performer Paul Winter and author/educator Marilyn Davidson contains 12 original and multicultural folk selections that pay tribute to all seven continents, plus the oceans, the mountains and the desert. The program promotes environmental awareness as it integrates arts and sciences.

(LG0019) Teacher's Guide
(LG0019AT) Teacher's Guide and Cassette
(LG0019CD) Teacher's Guide and CD

(LG0019S) Student Book
(LG0019B) Classroom Bundle (10% Savings)
Includes 1 Teacher's Guide; 25 Student Books; and
1 Earth: Voices of a Planet CD

Available from your favorite music dealer